BARE
Journal

inspired girl

Bare Companion Journal by Niccole Nelson

Published by Inspired Girl, an imprint of Inspired Girl Publishing Group, a subsidiary of Inspired Girl Enterprises
Asbury Park, NJ
www.inspiredgirlbooks.com

Inspired Girl is honored to bring forth books with heart and stories that matter. We are proud to offer this book to our readers; the story, the experiences, and the words are the author's alone.

The author and publisher do not assume and hereby disclaim any liability in connection with the use of the information contained in this book. The information presented is the author's opinion and does not constitute any health or medical advice. The content of this book is for informational purposes only and is not intended to diagnose, treat, cure, or prevent any mental or physical condition or disease. This book is not intended as a substitute for the medical advice of physicians, therapists, or counselors. The reader should regularly consult a professional in matters relating to their physical and mental health, particularly with respect to any symptoms that may require diagnosis or medical attention.

© 2025 Niccole Nelson

All rights reserved. No portion of this book may be reproduced in any form without permission from the publisher, except as permitted by U.S. copyright law. For permissions contact: help@inspiredgirlbooks.com

ISBN: 978-1-965240-18-2

Creative Direction by Jennifer Tuma-Young
Cover Design by Andrej Semnic
Typesetting by Roseanna White

Packaging and Editing by Inspired Girl Publishing Group

In *Bare*, my "Note from the author" has a line at the end that reads...

> *"However, there is no recovery without bringing your truth to the Light."*

The capital L in Light is not a typo. It is You. Your Light that you need to show up and off to the world. To illuminate a way for others as well. A way to burn away the things that have kept you from believing in your power.

I heard from so many of you that Bare was a guide. You wrote in the margins, dog-eared pages, and flipped it open to random sections for a daily dose of inspiration and encouragement. This moved me to design this companion journal so you could fill the pages beyond the margins and Bare it all!

DEDICATION

Bare *is dedicated to CoCo.*
My younger self. She is the reason I pray the way I do.
I'm proud of her for fighting for us.

This journal is for you to share what makes your younger self proud. How you have evolved through this journey of healing your inner child.

(START YOUR LETTER/DEDICATION TO YOUR YOUNGER SELF)

Dear _____,

_____
_____
_____
_____
_____
_____
_____
_____
_____
_____
_____
_____
_____
_____
_____
_____
_____
_____
_____
_____
_____

Signed,

DATE: _____

HOW ARE YOU USING YOUR LIGHT?

refer to Bare: Note from the Author pg. vii

_____
_____
_____
_____
_____
_____
_____
_____
_____
_____
_____
_____
_____
_____
_____
_____
_____
_____
_____
_____
_____
_____

SAY MORE NO'S TO LIVE A GREATER YES

DATE: _____

I WILL BE INTENTIONAL WITH MY BOUNDARIES

DATE: _____

WHEN IS A TIME YOU BET ON YOURSELF?

refer to Bare: Foreword pg. ix

_____
_____
_____
_____
_____
_____
_____
_____
_____
_____
_____
_____
_____
_____
_____
_____
_____
_____
_____
_____
_____

TIME IS MORE VALUABLE THAN MONEY,
AND I DON'T WASTE EITHER

DATE:

I WILL GIVE MYSELF GRACE

DATE: _____

WHAT HAVE YOU LAID BARE?
HOW HAVE YOU EVOLVED SINCE YOU DID?

> refer to Bare: Title Page

_____
_____
_____
_____
_____
_____
_____
_____
_____
_____
_____
_____
_____
_____
_____
_____
_____
_____
_____
_____
_____
_____
_____

HIDDEN TRUTH IS NOT HEALTHY

DATE:

OUTCOMES BELONG TO GOD

DATE: _____

YOU MAY FEEL TRIGGERED.
FIND SPACE WITHIN TO EXPLORE THE TRIGGER
AND MOVE THROUGH THE DISCOMFORT
TO OWNERSHIP OF YOUR LIFE AND PAST.

> refer to Bare: Trigger Warning

_____
_____
_____
_____
_____
_____
_____
_____
_____
_____
_____
_____
_____
_____
_____
_____
_____
_____
_____
_____

TRIGGERED WITH TOOLS MEANS YOU'RE TRIUMPHANT

DATE:

I AM SAFE

DATE: _____

REMEMBER YOUR INNER CHILD DESERVES YOUR LOVE AND IS PROUD OF YOU. WHAT DO YOU WANT TO SAY TO THEM TODAY?

> refer to Bare: Table of Contents

NEVER UNDERESTIMATE THE POWER OF YOUR INNER KID

DATE:

I HOLD SPACE FOR MYSELF

DATE: _____

WHO WILL BE BETTER BECAUSE YOU SHARED YOUR STORY?

> refer to Bare: Prelude: Past, Present and Purpose

_____
_____
_____
_____
_____
_____
_____
_____
_____
_____
_____
_____
_____
_____
_____
_____
_____
_____
_____
_____

YOUR VOICE HAS VALUE

DATE:

CONTROL IS AN ILLUSION

DATE: _____

WHAT EXERCISE DO YOU PRACTICE TO STRENGTHEN YOUR MIND TO BUILD MENTAL STAMINA?

> refer to Bare: Letting My Hair Down pg. 3

___

CASTING DOWN IMAGINATIONS AND EVERY HIGH THING THAT EXALTETH ITSELF AGAINST THE KNOWLEDGE OF GOD, AND BRINGING INTO CAPTIVITY EVERY THOUGHT TO THE OBEDIENCE OF CHRIST

DATE: _____

I HAVE UNLEARNED THE BEHAVIORS THAT KEPT ME STUCK IN
THE SPIRAL OF DISFUNCTION

DATE: _____

WHAT DO YOU NEED TO RELINQUISH CONTROL OF BECAUSE GOD DOESN'T NEED YOUR INPUT?

refer to Bare: Methods pg. 5

_____
_____
_____
_____
_____
_____
_____
_____
_____
_____
_____
_____
_____
_____
_____
_____
_____
_____
_____

"YOU HAVE A RESPONSIBILITY TO YOU TO BE WHOLE."
— GOD

DATE:

LOVE IS AVAILABLE TO ME

DATE: _____

WHAT DOES IT FEEL LIKE FOR YOU TO BE IN TOTAL ALIGNMENT?

refer to Bare: Survival Shift pg. 8

_____
_____
_____
_____
_____
_____
_____
_____
_____
_____
_____
_____
_____
_____
_____
_____
_____
_____
_____
_____

PEACE IS PURPOSEFUL POWER

DATE: _____

I USE MY FULL EMOTIONAL VOCABULARY

DATE: _____

WHAT HAVE YOU HAD TO UNLEARN?
> refer to Bare: Faith Without Works Is Dead pg. 10

_____

HOW WE SEE OURSELVES IS MOST IMPORTANT

DATE:

HEALING IS A LONG GAME

DATE: _____

WHAT COPING TOOLS HAVE YOU ADOPTED ON YOUR HEALING JOURNEY?

refer to Bare: White noise pg. 12

_____

KNOWING THE LESSON IS ONE THING,
GETTING IT IS ANOTHER

DATE:

I AM NOT A MISTAKE

DATE: _____

WHAT SERIES OF YOUR LIFE EVENTS DO YOU NEED TO STOP BINGING?

> refer to Bare: Old News pg. 15

_____
_____
_____
_____
_____
_____
_____
_____
_____
_____
_____
_____
_____
_____
_____
_____
_____
_____
_____
_____

YOU PRETENDED TO BE OKAY FOR SO LONG
YOU STARTED TO BELIEVE IT

DATE: _____

WHAT HAPPENED TO ME WAS WRONG.
I AM NOT WRONG.

DATE: _____

WHAT MOUNTAINS IN YOUR LIFE HAVE YOU BUILT AND/OR TORN DOWN?

refer to Bare: Mountain Mover pg. 18

**YOUR DOUBTS CREATE MOUNTAINS.
YOUR ACTIONS MOVE THEM.**

DATE:

I TAKE OWNERSHIP OF MY DECISIONS AND ACTIONS

DATE: _____

WHO IN YOUR LIFE TOUCHES YOUR HEART THROUGH MENTAL STIMULATION?

> refer to Bare: Mental Stimulation pg. 22

_____

SAPIOSEXUALS DO IT FOR ME

DATE: _____

CLARITY AND CONFIDENCE ARE MINE BECAUSE
I AM COMMITTED AND CONSISTENT

DATE: _____

WHO HAS YOUR LOVE HELPED HEAL?

refer to Bare: Medicinal pg. 24

___

READING IS A BALM TO MY SOUL

DATE: _____

I LET PEOPLE LOVE ME BECAUSE I AM WORTHY

DATE: _____

ARE YOU OPEN TO OR IN THERAPY? HOW HAS IT SHIFTED THE WAY YOU SEE YOURSELF?

> refer to Bare: Reality Check pg. 26

_____
_____
_____
_____
_____
_____
_____
_____
_____
_____
_____
_____
_____
_____
_____
_____
_____
_____
_____
_____

THIS BOOK IS THE THERAPY I NEVER HAD

DATE:

TODAY IS ALL I HAVE
SO NO NEED TO BE ANXIOUS ABOUT THE FUTURE

DATE: _____

HOW HAVE YOU OWNED YOUR POWER BY BEING COURAGEOUS?

> refer to Bare: Power Driver pg. 27

_____
_____
_____
_____
_____
_____
_____
_____
_____
_____
_____
_____
_____
_____
_____
_____
_____
_____
_____
_____
_____

POWER MEANS COURAGEOUS AND WISE

DATE: _____

WHEN I DO THE WORK, THE REWARD IS SO MUCH SWEETER

DATE: _____

HOW ARE YOU INTENTIONAL ABOUT KEEPING YOUR LIGHT BRIGHT?

refer to Bare: The Light pg. 29

_____

DON'T FORGET WHO YOU WERE BEFORE THE PAIN GOT IN

DATE: _____

FILLING MY CUP DAILY GIVES ME THE CAPACITY
TO LOVE AND TO SERVE

DATE: _____

WHAT DO YOU DO TO NOT BETRAY YOUR HEART, SHOWING OTHERS YOU ARE INHERENTLY WORTHY?

> refer to Bare: Unbuttoning My Blouse pg. 31

_____
_____
_____
_____
_____
_____
_____
_____
_____
_____
_____
_____
_____
_____
_____
_____
_____

KEEP YOUR PROMISES TO YOURSELF

DATE:

HEALTH MATTERS FROM HEAD TO TOE

DATE: _____

WHO DOES GOD SAY YOU ARE?

refer to Bare: Silent Killer pg. 33

_____
_____
_____
_____
_____
_____
_____
_____
_____
_____
_____
_____
_____
_____
_____
_____
_____
_____
_____
_____

BE THE VERSION OF YOURSELF GOD SEES

DATE: _____

TODAY I WILL CREATE A PLAYLIST FOR MY PURPOSE

DATE:

WHAT DO YOU BELIEVE YOU DESERVE?

refer to Bare: Prom Night pg. 35

THE FAIRY TALE IS YOURS

DATE:

LIFE HAS EBBS AND FLOWS. THERE IS NO NEED FOR ME TO
LABEL IT, I CAN JUST MOVE THROUGH IT

DATE: _____

HOW HAVE YOU BUILT SELF TRUST?

refer to Bare: Ships Passing pg. 36

_____
_____
_____
_____
_____
_____
_____
_____
_____
_____
_____
_____
_____
_____
_____
_____
_____
_____
_____
_____

TRUST GOD

DATE: _____

MY SUPPORT SYSTEM IS VETTED TO HOLD MY TRUTH

DATE: _____

WHERE ARE YOU PLAYING IT SAFE, BUT TRULY DESIRE MORE? HOW WILL YOU LEAVE YOUR COMFORT ZOME?

refer to Bare: Out of My Familiar pg. 38

_____
_____
_____
_____
_____
_____
_____
_____
_____
_____
_____
_____
_____
_____
_____
_____
_____
_____
_____
_____
_____

DON'T LET LOYALTY KEEP YOU FROM LEGACY

DATE: _____

THERE IS NOBODY ELSE THAT IS ME,
AND THERE NEVER WILL BE

DATE: _____

HOW HAS COPING CRIPPLED YOU AND WHAT DID YOU DO TO SHIFT?

refer to Bare: Coping pg. 41

_____
_____
_____
_____
_____
_____
_____
_____
_____
_____
_____
_____
_____
_____
_____
_____
_____
_____
_____
_____

GOD KEEPS HIS PROMISES

DATE:

BEING LIKED IS NOT A PREREQUISITE FOR ME TO BE MYSELF
AND BE HAPPY WITH WHO THAT IS

DATE: _____

WHAT WERE SOME CIRCLES OF EVENTS THAT CHANGED THE TRAJECTORY OF YOUR LIFE? HOW HAVE YOU NAVIGATED THAT?

> refer to Bare: Circle of Events pg. 45

_____
_____
_____
_____
_____
_____
_____
_____
_____
_____
_____
_____
_____
_____
_____
_____
_____
_____
_____

LIFE CHANGES IN THE BLINK OF AN EYE. BE GRATEFUL.

DATE:

COMBAT EVERY LIE FROM THE ENEMY
WITH THE TRUTH OF GOD'S WORD

DATE: _____

HOW HAVE YOU HAD TO REBUILD TRUST?

refer to Bare: The Side You Don't See pg. 47

_____
_____
_____
_____
_____
_____
_____
_____
_____
_____
_____
_____
_____
_____
_____
_____
_____
_____
_____
_____
_____
_____
_____

DAILY DECISIONS DETERMINE OUR LIFE

DATE:

FAILING IS HOW I FIND MY FREEDOM,
NOT SOMETHING THAT KEEPS ME FROM IT

DATE: _____

WHAT IS A CHILDHOOD OR PLAYFUL MEMORY THAT BRINGS YOU JOY?
refer to Bare: Earth, Bricks, and Boxes pg. 52

DON'T FORGET TO PLAY

DATE:

WHAT IF IT ALL WORKS OUT?

DATE: _____

HOW DO YOU RESTORE?
WHAT DID YOU DO TODAY FOR YOURSELF?

refer to Bare: Self pg. 54

_____
_____
_____
_____
_____
_____
_____
_____
_____
_____
_____
_____
_____
_____
_____
_____
_____
_____
_____
_____
_____
_____

NEVER LEAVE YOU OFF YOUR LIST

DATE:

I AM COURAGEOUS

DATE: _____

HOW HAS EMPATHY PLAYED OUT IN YOUR OWN STORY?

refer to Bare: Heroine pg. 56

_____
_____
_____
_____
_____
_____
_____
_____
_____
_____
_____
_____
_____
_____
_____
_____
_____
_____
_____
_____
_____

SECOND CHANCES ARE EXPENSIVE

DATE: _____

IT'S ONLY LEFT UP TO CHANCE IF I DON'T TAKE ONE

DATE: _____

WHEN IN YOUR LIFE HAS RETAIL THERAPY PLAYED A ROLE IN YOUR HEALING?

> refer to Bare: Clearance Jack pg. 58

_____
_____
_____
_____
_____
_____
_____
_____
_____
_____
_____
_____
_____
_____
_____
_____
_____
_____
_____
_____

DON'T DISCOUNT YOUR LOVE

DATE: _____

_____

I ACCEPT THE INVITATION OF THE UNKNOWN AS AN
ADVENTURE TO SEE WHAT'S POSSIBLE

DATE: _____

NO ONE CAN TELL ANYONE HOW TO GRIEVE. WHAT HAVE BEEN WAYS YOU HAVE MANAGED GRIEF?

> refer to Bare: Missing Mom pg. 60

_____
_____
_____
_____
_____
_____
_____
_____
_____
_____
_____
_____
_____
_____
_____
_____
_____
_____
_____
_____

SOMETIMES HEALTHY HURTS

DATE:

I TRUST MY INNER GUIDE

DATE: _____

IF YOU ARE A PARENT, WHAT ROLE HAS YOUR CHILD'S/CHILDREN'S LOVE PLAYED IN YOUR JOURNEY OF GROWTH, HEALING AND EVOLUTION?

> refer to Bare: The 3 People God Let Invade My Heart pg. 62

_____
_____
_____
_____
_____
_____
_____
_____
_____
_____
_____
_____
_____
_____
_____
_____
_____

LET PEOPLE LOVE YOU

DATE:

FOR HE IS GOOD
FOR HIS MERCY ENDURES FOREVER

DATE: _____

WHEN IN YOUR LIFE HAVE YOU BEEN AUDACIOUS?

refer to Bare: What's in Her Name pg. 66

_____
_____
_____
_____
_____
_____
_____
_____
_____
_____
_____
_____
_____
_____
_____
_____
_____
_____
_____
_____

LIVE LIFE EXTREMELY BOLD

DATE: _____

AS MY TITLES AND ROLES CHANGE MY CORE WILL REMAIN
SOLID WITH EVERY EVOLUTION

DATE: _____

WHAT OR WHO BRINGS BEAUTY TO YOUR LIFE?

refer to Bare: The Beauty of My Baby pg. 69

_____
_____
_____
_____
_____
_____
_____
_____
_____
_____
_____
_____
_____
_____
_____
_____
_____
_____
_____
_____

LOOK UP FROM LIFE FROM TIME TO TIME

DATE:

NEVER HIDE YOUR LIGHT

DATE: _____

HOW ARE YOU TAKING CENTER STAGE IN YOUR OWN LIFE?

refer to Bare: Center Stage pg. 72

_____
_____
_____
_____
_____
_____
_____
_____
_____
_____
_____
_____
_____
_____
_____
_____
_____
_____
_____
_____
_____

I WILL NEVER BE WITHOUT LOVE
AS LONG AS I HAVE IT FOR MYSELF

DATE: _____

JESUS CALLS ME FRIEND

DATE: _____

WHAT RELATIONSHIP(S) HAVE YOU NEEDED? HOW HAS IT BLESSED YOU?

refer to Bare: MEN-ding pg. 75

_____
_____
_____
_____
_____
_____
_____
_____
_____
_____
_____
_____
_____
_____
_____
_____
_____
_____
_____

A VILLAGE IS VALUABLE

DATE:

THE BEAUTY FOR ASHES ONLY COMES AFTER THE BATTLE

DATE: _____

WHOSE PERMISSION ARE YOU WAITING FOR TO LIVE, BE, DO, OR SAY WHAT GOD WANTS YOU TO BE, DO, OR SAY? WHOSE DO YOU ACTUALLY NEED?

> refer to Bare: Hide and Seek pg. 76

I HAVE NOTHING LESS THAN MAIN CHARACTER ENERGY

DATE:

THERE IS NO RESTORATION WITHOUT REST

DATE: _____

WHOSE VOICE DO YOU NEED TO SILENCE TO HEAR YOURS AND GODS CLEARLY?

> refer to Bare: One Word from God pg. 77

_____
_____
_____
_____
_____
_____
_____
_____
_____
_____
_____
_____
_____
_____
_____
_____
_____
_____
_____
_____
_____

MY VOICE MATTERS

DATE:

BE GENTLE WITH YOURSELF

DATE: _____

IS THERE ANYWHERE IN YOUR LIFE THAT YOU'RE HIDING?
WHAT WOULD HAPPEN IF YOU STOPPED?

refer to Bare: Within pg. 79

_____
_____
_____
_____
_____
_____
_____
_____
_____
_____
_____
_____
_____
_____
_____
_____
_____
_____
_____

SHOW UP

DATE: _____

YOUR TEARS MATTER TO GOD

DATE: _____

WHEN WE SAY YES TO THINGS WE WANTED TO OR SHOULD'VE SAID NO TO, RESENTMENT SETS IN. IS THERE ANYWHERE YOU'RE COMPROMISING YOUR PEACE FOR SOMEONE ELSE'S COMFORT? WHAT WOULD YOU ENJOY IF YOU STOPPED?

refer to Bare: Diminished pg. 80

NEVER BREAK YOUR OWN HEART

DATE:

DON'T LET ANYONE ELSE'S VOICE
BE LOUDER THAN YOURS OR GOD'S

DATE: _____

HOW ARE YOU TEACHING PEOPLE HOW TO LOVE YOU? IS IT WHAT YOU WANT?

> refer to Bare: Remnants pg. 82

___

I'M NOT GONNA IGNORE MY GUT, BUT I'M NOT GONNA TALK MYSELF OUT OF LOVE ANYMORE

DATE: _____

WHAT I BELIEVE DETERMINES WHO I BECOME,
NOT WHAT I DO

DATE: _____

WHAT ROOTS OF PAIN HAS GOD HAD TO DIG UP FOR YOU?

refer to Bare: Daddy Issues pg. 84

_____
_____
_____
_____
_____
_____
_____
_____
_____
_____
_____
_____
_____
_____
_____
_____
_____
_____
_____
_____
_____

NURTURE YOURSELF THROUGH THE EVOLUTION

DATE:

WHAT WILL SERVE MY HIGHEST GOOD?

DATE: _____

HOW ARE YOU PARTNERING WITH GOD TO PLAY THE HAND YOU'VE BEEN DEALT?

refer to Bare: Spades pg. 85

_____
_____
_____
_____
_____
_____
_____
_____
_____
_____
_____
_____
_____
_____
_____
_____
_____
_____
_____
_____

IT'S NOT THE CARDS YOU'RE DEALT
BUT HOW YOU PLAY THE HAND

DATE: _____

DON'T LET GOOD KEEP YOU FROM GREAT

DATE: _____

WHAT IS SOMETHING YOU BLOTTED OUT OR WISHED YOU COULD?
HOW DO YOU FEEL HAVING NOW PROCESSED WHAT YOU WITNESSED?

> refer to Bare: Witness pg. 86

_____

MAKE MOVES FROM VISION, NOT SIGHT

DATE: _____

PRAYER IS WHERE WARRIORS RECEIVE
THE STRATEGY FOR WAR

DATE: _____

WHAT CHOICES HAVE YOU MADE IN SURVIVAL MODE THAT YOU'RE GLAD TO LEAVE BEHIND?

> refer to Bare: Choices pg. 89

_____

_____

_____

_____

_____

_____

_____

_____

_____

_____

_____

_____

_____

_____

_____

_____

_____

_____

CHOOSE TO THRIVE

DATE: _____

PEOPLE, PLACES, AND THINGS THAT NO LONGER SERVE ME
HAVE NO PLACE IN MY LIFE

DATE: _____

HOW DO YOU PRACTICE RADICAL SELF ACCEPTANCE?

> refer to Bare: Someone to Love pg. 90

_____
_____
_____
_____
_____
_____
_____
_____
_____
_____
_____
_____
_____
_____
_____
_____
_____
_____
_____
_____

YOU MATTER

DATE: _____

MY NERVOUS SYSTEM IS REGULATED

DATE: _____

WHAT IMAGE DO YOU HAVE OF YOUR SELF?

refer to Bare: Images pg. 92

_____
_____
_____
_____
_____
_____
_____
_____
_____
_____
_____
_____
_____
_____
_____
_____
_____
_____
_____
_____
_____

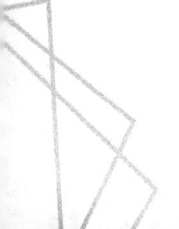

MAKE GOOD MEMORIES

DATE:

I SURROUND MYSELF WITH LOVE

DATE: _____

HOW ARE YOU INTENTIONAL IN YOUR ROMANTIC RELATIONSHIP?

> refer to Bare: Head PSA pg. 93

_____

HOW YOU COMMUNICATE AT THE TABLE
IS AS IMPORTANT AS WHAT YOU BRING TO IT

DATE: _____

I TAKE FULL CREDIT FOR MY YES

DATE: _____

HOW COMFORTABLE ARE YOU WITH INTIMACY IN AND OUTSIDE OF THE BEDROOM?

> refer to Bare: Chemistry pg. 96

_____
_____
_____
_____
_____
_____
_____
_____
_____
_____
_____
_____
_____
_____
_____
_____
_____
_____
_____
_____

ATTENTION IS NOT LOVE

DATE: _____

I AM DESIRABLE

DATE: _____

WHO OR WHAT HAVE YOU DESIRED, BUT KNEW OR BELIEVED YOU WEREN'T READY FOR SO YOU LET IT/THEM GO?

refer to Bare: Distant Lover pg. 98

_____
_____
_____
_____
_____
_____
_____
_____
_____
_____
_____
_____
_____
_____
_____
_____
_____
_____
_____
_____
_____

BEING BRAVE ISN'T ALWAYS ABOUT DOING—
SOMETIMES IT'S ABOUT STOPPING

DATE:

I CAN HEAL AND SERVE AT THE SAME TIME

DATE: _____

WHAT DOES ABUNDANCE LOOK LIKE IN YOUR LIFE?

refer to Bare: Lack-A-Doodle-Do pg. 100

_____
_____
_____
_____
_____
_____
_____
_____
_____
_____
_____
_____
_____
_____
_____
_____
_____
_____
_____
_____

YOUR BANK ACCOUNT IS NOT YOUR IDENTITY

DATE:

GOD HAS PROMISES FOR YOU

DATE: _____

BROKEN DOESN'T MEAN BAD.
WHAT YOU BELIEVE IS WHAT MATTERS.
HOW HAVE YOU BEEN MORE OPEN TO
LOVE BEYOND YOUR PAST?

refer to Bare: Love of the Broken pg. 102

_____
_____
_____
_____
_____
_____
_____
_____
_____
_____
_____
_____
_____
_____
_____
_____
_____
_____
_____
_____
_____

LOVE LEAVES ROOM FOR RESTORATION

DATE: _____

YOU'VE ALWAYS BEEN ENOUGH

DATE: _____

HOW HAVE YOUR WOUNDS
GIVEN YOU WISDOM?

refer to Bare: Removing my Bra pg. 105

_____
_____
_____
_____
_____
_____
_____
_____
_____
_____
_____
_____
_____
_____
_____
_____
_____
_____
_____
_____
_____

WHAT YOU LEARN FROM YOU CAN LEVERAGE

DATE:

I AM MINDFUL OF HOW I SPEND MY TIME

DATE: _____

HOW DO YOU SELF SOOTHE?

refer to Bare: Battle Scars pg.107

_____
_____
_____
_____
_____
_____
_____
_____
_____
_____
_____
_____
_____
_____
_____
_____
_____
_____
_____
_____
_____
_____

PERFECTION IS NOT A REQUIREMENT TO GAIN ACCESS TO GOD'S PROMISES. AMEN.

DATE: _____

I TRUST MYSELF

DATE: _____

WHAT'S A LITTLE THING YOU CAN DO OR CHANGE TODAY THAT FUTURE YOU WILL THANK YOU FOR?

> refer to Bare: Contract pg. 109

_____
_____
_____
_____
_____
_____
_____
_____
_____
_____
_____
_____
_____
_____
_____
_____
_____
_____
_____

I AM VALUABLE

DATE: _____

GOD ALWAYS SEES YOU AT YOUR BEST

DATE: _____

WHERE ARE YOU PUTTING SKIN IN THE GAME?

refer to Bare: Battle Fatigue pg. 112

_____

I AM WORTH THE INVESTMENT

DATE: _____

GOD KEEPS CONFIRMING HIS LOVE IS TRUE

DATE: _____

WHAT LIE ABOUT YOURSELF HAVE YOU TURNED ON IT'S HEAD?

> refer to Bare: Wrong Truth or Wrong Lie pg. 113

_____
_____
_____
_____
_____
_____
_____
_____
_____
_____
_____
_____
_____
_____
_____
_____
_____
_____
_____

I WAS BORN TO SHINE

DATE:

MY BODY IS A BLESSING

DATE: _____

WHAT ARE YOU MOST EXCITED ABOUT LETTING GO OF NOW LEAVING SURVIVAL MODE?

> refer to Bare: Pick Your Poison pg. 115

_____
_____
_____
_____
_____
_____
_____
_____
_____
_____
_____
_____
_____
_____
_____
_____
_____
_____
_____

I AM HEALED

DATE: _____

LIFE CAN CHANGE IN A MOMENT.
BE PRESENT FOR THEM ALL.

DATE: _____

JUST BE.

refer to Bare: Being pg. 117

I'M THE WOMAN WHO WILL SHOW YOU HOW TO GET
THE VICTORY IN THE VALLEY

DATE: _____

THE MORE I HEAL, THE BRIGHTER MY LIGHT BECOMES

DATE: _____

HOW DO YOU VALUE AND HONOR YOUR BODY?

refer to Bare: Sliding off My Panties pg. 119

_____
_____
_____
_____
_____
_____
_____
_____
_____
_____
_____
_____
_____
_____
_____
_____
_____
_____
_____
_____

I AM MY BEST ADVOCATE

DATE:

ALL THE PARTS OF YOU MAKE A MASTERPIECE

DATE: _____

WHAT EVENT DID YOU BEGIN TO ACCEPT AS IDENTITY, THAT WAS FALSE?

refer to Bare: Sleight of Hand pg. 121

_____
_____
_____
_____
_____
_____
_____
_____
_____
_____
_____
_____
_____
_____
_____
_____
_____
_____
_____
_____

WHAT HAPPENED TO ME IS NOT WHO I AM

DATE:

THE THING YOU'RE HIDING
IS THE THING GOD WANTS TO USE

DATE: _____

HOW HAVE/WILL YOU CELEBRATE YOURSELF FOR NO LONGER HIDING?

> refer to Bare: Labor Pains pg. 122

_____
_____
_____
_____
_____
_____
_____
_____
_____
_____
_____
_____
_____
_____
_____
_____
_____
_____
_____
_____

I AM A BEAUTIFUL EXAMPLE

DATE: _____

I ASK FOR HELP

DATE: _____

SHARE A TIME YOU CHOSE YOU.

> refer to Bare: Chocolate Chip Cookies vs. Oreos pg. 124

I AM WORTHY

DATE: _____

LET PEOPLE POUR INTO YOU
SO YOU HAVE MORE TO POUR OUT

DATE: _____

HOW DOES SHARING YOUR TRUTH HELP YOU REBUILD TRUST IN PEOPLE?

refer to Bare: The First pg. 126

_____
_____
_____
_____
_____
_____
_____
_____
_____
_____
_____
_____
_____
_____
_____
_____
_____
_____

I FORGIVE MYSELF FOR WHAT I BELIEVED WAS MY FAULT, BUT WASN'T

DATE:

GOD WILL NEVER LEAVE ME BROKEN

DATE: _____

WHEN WAS THERE A TIME YOU TOOK YOUR POWER BACK?

refer to Bare: Truer Words Never Spoken pg. 127

_____
_____
_____
_____
_____
_____
_____
_____
_____
_____
_____
_____
_____
_____
_____
_____
_____
_____
_____
_____

NO SETTLING

DATE: _____

FEELINGS ARE NOT FACTS BUT THEY ARE VALID

DATE: _____

WHAT'S YOUR FAVORITE FOOD?

refer to Bare: Mac 'N Cheese
and Cornbread pg. 128

_____
_____
_____
_____
_____
_____
_____
_____
_____
_____
_____
_____
_____
_____
_____
_____
_____
_____
_____

I ENJOY ALL THE DELICIOUSNESS OF MY LIFE

DATE:

I SHOW UP IN EXCELLENCE

DATE: _____

HOW HAS DEEPENING YOUR RELATIONSHIP WITH GOD HELPED YOU MOVE THROUGH THE DISCOMFORT OF HEALING?

> refer to Bare: Dazed and Confused pg. 131

_____
_____
_____
_____
_____
_____
_____
_____
_____
_____
_____
_____
_____
_____
_____
_____
_____
_____
_____
_____

LOVE DOESN'T INCLUDE SHAME

DATE:

I AM ON ASSIGNMENT

DATE: _____

HOW ARE YOU GIVING OTHERS THE COURAGE TO SHARE THEIR STORY?

refer to Bare: School Clothes pg. 132

_____
_____
_____
_____
_____
_____
_____
_____
_____
_____
_____
_____
_____
_____
_____
_____
_____
_____
_____
_____

YOU DESERVE LOVE AND PHYSICAL TOUCH IN A SAFE, TRUSTING, CONSENSUAL MANNER

DATE:

PURPOSE OVER POPULAR

DATE: _____

WHAT'S YOUR F-THAT MOMENT/THOUGHT?

> refer to Bare: F-that! pg. 135

_____
_____
_____
_____
_____
_____
_____
_____
_____
_____
_____
_____
_____
_____
_____
_____
_____
_____

I OWN MY BODY

DATE:

EVEN WHEN I AM AT A DEFICIT, I AM NOT DEFEATED

DATE: _____

HOW DO YOU EXPRESS YOUR ANGER?

refer to Bare: Anger Be Damned, This Is Rage pg. 136

ANGER IS NOT WRONG

DATE:

I WILL PLAY FULL OUT AND LEAVE EMPTY

DATE: _____

WHAT FEELS SO GOOD TO YOU THAT IT FEELS LIKE YOU'RE PROGRAMMED TO ENJOY IT?

> refer to Bare: Virtual Orgasm pg. 139

___

MY LIFE IS FILLED WITH PLEASURE

DATE: _____

GOD CAN PUT A DEMAND ON WHAT I POSSESS

DATE: _____

WHERE IS GOD GUIDING YOU NEXT?

refer to Bare: Taking Shoes and Socks Off! pg. 141

_____
_____
_____
_____
_____
_____
_____
_____
_____
_____
_____
_____
_____
_____
_____
_____
_____
_____
_____
_____

MY FUTURE IS BRIGHT AND HAS NO ANXIETY

DATE: _____

I AM OPEN TO WHAT GOD WANTS TO DO WITH AND IN ME

DATE: _____

HOW DOES PRESENTING YOUR BEST EVERYDAY, HELP OTHERS SHOW UP AS THEIRS?

refer to Bare: You & Them pg. 143

_____
_____
_____
_____
_____
_____
_____
_____
_____
_____
_____
_____
_____
_____
_____
_____
_____
_____
_____
_____
_____
_____

I AM A REFLECTION OF GRACE

DATE: _____

DON'T DOUBT THE DIVINE WITHIN YOU

DATE: _____

HOW HAVE YOU MOVED FROM MERELY EXISTING TO LIVING?

> refer to Bare: Saved and Bound pg. 144

_____
_____
_____
_____
_____
_____
_____
_____
_____
_____
_____
_____
_____
_____
_____
_____
_____
_____
_____
_____

I AM FREE TO BE WHO GOD DESIGNED ME TO BE

DATE: _____

MY WILDEST DREAMS ARE COMING TRUE

DATE: _____

HOW DO YOU STAY PRESENT IN THE MOMENT?

> refer to Bare: Nip and Tuck pg. 146

_____
_____
_____
_____
_____
_____
_____
_____
_____
_____
_____
_____
_____
_____
_____
_____
_____
_____
_____
_____

I'M IN MY LANE AND WINNING

DATE: _____

SAVOR ALL THE MOMENTS OF LIFE

DATE: _____

WHAT HAS GOD BEEN CALLING YOU TO THAT YOU'VE BEEN IGNORING/AVOIDING BECAUSE YOU'RE NOT WHO YOU BELIEVE YOU NEED TO BE TO ACHIEVE IT? WHEN WILL YOU TAKE ACTION?

> refer to Bare: Can I Get an Upgrade? pg. 148

_____
_____
_____
_____
_____
_____
_____
_____
_____
_____
_____
_____
_____
_____
_____
_____
_____

I WANT TO EXPERIENCE LIFE ON A LEVEL I NEVER GAVE MYSELF PERMISSION TO ENJOY

DATE: _____

I WILL NOT HIDE IN MY TITLES AS A WAY TO ESCAPE

DATE: _____

WHAT IS YOUR FAVORITE FORM OF CREATIVE EXPRESSION?

refer to Bare: To the Artist pg. 152

_____
_____
_____
_____
_____
_____
_____
_____
_____
_____
_____
_____
_____
_____
_____
_____
_____
_____
_____
_____
_____

THE EVOLUTION OF ME IS ONE THAT I BELIEVE IS AND
WILL BE MY GREATEST ADVENTURE

DATE:

I AM HEALTHY SPIRITUATLLY, MENTALLY,
EMOTIONALLY, AND PHYSICALLY

DATE: _____

DID YOU FALL FOR THE TRAP OF MULTI-TASKING?
WHEN DID YOU REALIZE IT?

> refer to Bare: One At a Time pg. 155

_____
_____
_____
_____
_____
_____
_____
_____
_____
_____
_____
_____
_____
_____
_____
_____
_____
_____
_____
_____

WHAT I'VE HAD AND WHAT I DESERVE HAVE BEEN TWO VERY DIFFERENT THINGS. I'M COMING TO COLLECT!

DATE:

I AM A GOOD STEWARD OF MY BLESSINGS

DATE: _____

HOW ARE YOU EXPERIENCING A WELL-LIVED LIFE?

refer to Bare: Resurrection pg. 157

_____
_____
_____
_____
_____
_____
_____
_____
_____
_____
_____
_____
_____
_____
_____
_____
_____
_____
_____
_____
_____

FATE: FOREVER ALIGNED TO ETERNITY

DATE: _____

I AM IN TOUCH WITH MY EMOTIONS
AND I CAN EXPRESS THEM WELL

DATE: _____

HOW DO YOU BREATHE THROUGH THE GRIEF OF CHANGE?

refer to Bare: Evolution Revolution pg. 158

_____

THE CHAINS HAVE FALLEN OFF. NOW I'M JUST TRYING TO
LEARN HOW TO WALK IN THIS NEW FREEDOM.

DATE:

PROTECT YOUR PEACE AT ALL COSTS

DATE: _____

HOW DO YOU COMBAT NEGATIVE SELF TALK AND MENTAL CLUTTER?

> refer to Bare: Weed Whacker pg. 159

_____
_____
_____
_____
_____
_____
_____
_____
_____
_____
_____
_____
_____
_____
_____
_____
_____
_____
_____
_____

IT WAS A MISTAKE. I AM NOT A MISTAKE.

DATE: _____

REMEMBER THOSE COMING BEHIND YOU

DATE: _____

WHAT DO YOU WANT TO BE KNOWN FOR?

> refer to Bare: Why I Spit pg. 160

I AM BRILLIANT AND I DON'T HAVE TO APOLOGIZE FOR IT

DATE:

YOU ARE THE DAUGHTER OF THE KING

DATE: _____

WHAT DO YOU WANT PEOPLE TO KNOW ABOUT YOU BEYOND YOUR TITLES?

> refer to Bare: Dropping Accessories pg. 163

_____
_____
_____
_____
_____
_____
_____
_____
_____
_____
_____
_____
_____
_____
_____
_____
_____
_____
_____
_____
_____

I AM FOCUSED ON MY FREEDOM

DATE:

SHOW YOURSELF KINDNESS

DATE: _____

WHAT ARE 3 THINGS YOU HAD TO UNLEARN?

refer to Bare: Mirror pg. 165

_____
_____
_____
_____
_____
_____
_____
_____
_____
_____
_____
_____
_____
_____
_____
_____
_____
_____
_____
_____

TRUE CHANGE HAPPENS WITHIN

DATE: _____

YOU ARE NOT A BURDEN
YOU ARE A BLESSING

DATE: _____

IN WHAT SITUATION WERE YOU TRYING TO CONTROL THE OUTCOME? HOW DID IT WORK OUT ONCE YOU LET GO OF CONTROL?

refer to Bare: Really, Though? pg. 166

_____
_____
_____
_____
_____
_____
_____
_____
_____
_____
_____
_____
_____
_____
_____
_____
_____
_____
_____

GOD IS MY GUIDE

DATE:

THE REFINER'S FIRE IS UNCOMFORTABLE BUT BENEFICIAL

DATE: _____

HOW ARE YOU PUTTING FAITH TO ACTION?
refer to Bare: Power Play pg. 167

_____
_____
_____
_____
_____
_____
_____
_____
_____
_____
_____
_____
_____
_____
_____
_____
_____
_____
_____
_____

EVEN IF YOU CAN'T FIGURE OUT WHO YOU ARE,
REMEMBER WHOSE YOU ARE

DATE:

OBEDIENCE TO GOD IS KEY TO THE SHIFT YOU DESIRE

DATE: _____

DISSOCIATION IS A TYPE OF UNCONSCIOUS DEFENSE MECHANISM THAT YOUR BRAIN USES TO PROTECT YOU FROM EMOTIONAL PAIN. IT INVOLVES DETACHING YOURSELF FROM REALITY AND CAN CAUSE TEMPORARY MEMORY LOSS. TRAUMA CAN ALSO AFFECT YOUR AUTOBIOGRAPHIC MEMORY. I DETACHED FROM MY LIFE. I SPOKE ABOUT MY LIFE AS IF I WAS AN OBSERVER EVEN AFTER THE THREAT WAS GONE. HAVE YOU EXPERIENCED ANYTHING LIKE THIS?

refer to Bare: Hiding in Plain Sight pg. 169

HE WILL LEAD YOU TO ALL TRUTH,
EVEN THE TRUTH ABOUT YOU

DATE: _____

LEAN INTO THE QUIET AND STILLNESS THAT IS NEEDED
TO MAKE THE MENTAL AND EMOTIONAL SHIFT FOR HEALING

DATE: _____

WHO ARE YOU AT YOUR CORE?
refer to Bare: His pg. 170

_____
_____
_____
_____
_____
_____
_____
_____
_____
_____
_____
_____
_____
_____
_____
_____
_____
_____
_____

I AM FREE AND VALUABLE

DATE: _____

DON'T GET SO FAMILIAR THAT YOU CAN'T LOOK WITH FRESH
EYES AT A PERSON, PLACE, OR SITUATION

DATE: _____

ASK GOD WHAT HIS VISION IS FOR YOUR LIFE.

> refer to Bare: God's View pg. 172

_____
_____
_____
_____
_____
_____
_____
_____
_____
_____
_____
_____
_____
_____
_____
_____
_____
_____
_____
_____
_____
_____
_____

WHAT GOD HAS DESIGNED FOR ME
IS BEYOND MY WILDEST DREAMS

DATE: _____

WHEN YOU SEEK GOD'S CHARACTER,
HIS HEART AND HANDS ARE SURE TO FOLLOW

DATE: _____

AS YOU REFLECT, WHO WILL YOU SHOW UP AS FROM NOW ON TO LIVE OUT YOUR PURPOSE?

refer to Bare: Rinse and Reflect pg. 173

DON'T KEEP THE SECRET!

DATE: _____

YOUR LEGACY WILL BE THE EVIDENCE OF YOUR FAITH

To learn more about Niccole Nelson or to order a copy of *Bare*, visit her website niccolenelson.com

www.ingramcontent.com/pod-product-compliance
Lightning Source LLC
Chambersburg PA
CBHW021156160426
43194CB00007B/767